AF535104

Love Letters

is an unusual modern love story, told entirely through the vehicle of an exchange of letters between two young lovers. They have been together—and now they are hundreds of miles apart, forced to continue their relationship by mail.

One reviewer described their relationship as "Love letters that challenge all our assumptions. In a society where relationships are based on getting rather than giving, these love letters pry open the lid of a more fulfilling alternative."

Another said that this book is "A must for those about to fall in love . . . a series of love letters that strike at the heart."

The author, Ann Warren, was formerly a writer for the British Broadcasting Corporation, and is now a pastoral counselor and free-lance journalist. She is married and has three children. Mrs. Warren holds an M.A. in Psychology, English, and History from St. Andrews University in Great Britain.

Love Letters

Ann Warren

WORD BOOKS
PUBLISHER
4800 WEST WACO DRIVE
WACO, TEXAS
76703

ISBN 0–8499–0263–0

Library of Congress Catalog Card Number: 80–50378

First published in Great Britain by Scripture Union.

Printed in the United States of America

London February 11th.

Dearest John,

Since you left last week, I feel completely lost. I never knew how much you meant to me before. There were always other friends to find & another new day. The loneliest place to me now is a crowd with hundreds of busy, unknown faces milling around me & scarcely one who stops to notice me or even give me a smile. I feel so empty & alone. I even catch myself wondering what I'm here for & why we bother with life at all!

It's all right, I'm not getting at you. I know you had to go back to Scotland, & I still feel partly responsible that college down here didn't work out for you. We spent so much time together, & it can't have done your studies any good. I had no idea it would mean that if you failed your exams again last term you might actually have to leave! I know you talked about it once or twice, but it never really sank in that these exams were <u>so</u> important — nothing seemed to matter while we were together, & now I feel so selfish, as if I've messed up your whole life without even thinking about it.

It was awful watching you trying to get almost any kind of a job just to stay & be with me, & knowing all the time how much you hated working on the roads & washing up piles of greasy plates in that grotty restuarant. I feel angry with your parents for not going on paying for the flat & insisting that you went home, but then I guess they have a right to - it's their money

& I suppose they felt it was being wasted. Probably they think I'm some kind of a bad influence too!

I tried phoning you last night (it took me a long time to pluck up the courage), and then I felt terrible when your father answered. He was quite polite until he realized who I was, & then informed me, in a very icy voice, that you were out. I wonder if he told you I rang?! I'm not sure I've got the courage to try that again — I hate the phone anyway. It's all right if I know for certain you are going to be on the other end, but then I don't, do I?

Oh John, I feel so lonely tonight –
I wish so much you were here
to put your arms around me
& make me feel safe again.

All my love,
Jackie. XXXX♡XXX

Gareloch February 15th.

Dear Jackie,

It was good to get your letter and better still to know that you really miss me. I think of you such a lot, and I suppose like you, I'm only now beginning to realise how much a part of my life you've been these past months. Every time I turn a new corner or sit at a park bench I half expect to see you walking towards me. Yesterday I saw a girl with fair hair, and wearing a red scarf, just like you – for a moment – and then I could hardly bear the emptiness.

Then there's the mess I've made of my life. Dad says there's no chance now of my getting a proper training up here. With my record no one will take me on. I hate him for saying it, but at the same time I know it's true. So, there's all that I've thrown down the drain without even realising what I was doing, and the trouble is, for me, it's my whole life! I never thought much about a career before, but now I realise that without one I'm pretty well stuck before I've started. You'll be all right, somehow I know you'll always cope, but for me it's really all over and done with before I've begun. I'm not going to let you take the blame; after all, I'm my own responsibility, but, like you, I just didn't realise the trouble we were getting ourselves into, and the mess I've made of it all! I just don't feel I know what life is supposed to be about any more.

I want so much to talk to you, to hold you, and share all our troubles. I'd like to phone you, but it's so difficult here with my mother hanging around trying to listen. Whoever I ring she always wants to know all about it, and they're so edgy about you at the moment it just doesn't seem worth the hassle – and I just haven't got the cash to go down to the phone box and feed in the 10p's!

Let's just write to one another for a bit – at least it feels a bit closer than sheer emptiness. It's so lovely to get your letters.

All my love,

John.

London
February 19th.

Dearest John,

Reading your letter I feel really terrible for both of us. It doesn't seem possible that just a few wonderful months of love could end this way. I have a great aching void inside me, & the same question keeps going through my head: what is life all about anyway? What are we here for? It all seems like some crazy game of chess over which we have no control. Yesterday some boring guy at the office was going on & on about the pointlessness of everything — that a hydrogen bomb was going to blow us all up anyway. We were just tiny specks of dust with no meaning; we might as well end it all now. I wanted to tell him to shut up – it was all beginning to make too much sense – then someone else did it for me. She's a quiet little thing, but I've noticed she always has a feeling of peace about her, & there's a sort of calm, comfortable atmosphere when she's around. She just said something about there being a much greater meaning to life than we all realised, that we had to look for it if we really wanted to find the answer. Most of the others laughed, but something in me wanted to ask her what she was talking about, when it was all over, though, I was too depressed to make the effort! All the same, she gave me a funny look as if she understood where I was.

Darling, I'm sorry I'm rambling on like this. It's just that I've got no answers. Yesterday it seemed as if our love for one another was the only thing on earth that mattered, but now it's suddenly changed & I don't know where I'm going! It was horrible last night at the disco without you! Now you're not here so many of those boys that used to make eyes at me before seem to think I'm up for sale to the highest bidder. Too many of the songs at the disco meant too much to me as well & I had to get out, but even then one of the boys followed me home, & I was really glad to get inside & bolt the door. Then there's this other thing, darling – I miss you so much in bed beside me. You know how we talked a lot about that before we ever did it, but honestly, I think it's the most terrible loss of all. I hope you won't take it the wrong way, when I say that I'm beginning to wish that we'd never started sleeping together. I know we've always said that we loved each other too much not to, but I always had a deep-down feeling that it was wrong, & now it's hit me more than I can say. My whole body seems to ache for you, & I almost find myself wondering if any man wouldn't be better than this great aching emptiness, this loneliness in bed, & everything in me reacts against that need. I'm sorry to write like this darling, I know it must hurt you, but I hurt myself right now, & I don't really feel too well either. Rather tired & sick most of the time. Oh, John, I wish you were here! Forgive me darling.

Lots of love,

Jackie. xx

Gareloch February 22nd.

Darling Jackie,

I really <u>am</u> sorry. I know I persuaded you into that. But we shared so much together it seemed the natural thing to do. With other girls it always seemed what they expected, and maybe a bit too easy, but for us it was different, it was special, at least it was for me. We slept together because we loved each other – and it really expressed something about us. Maybe if I'd thought about us being apart like this I would have done differently, but honestly, I don't think I would. And now I can hardly bear to hear you talk like that about other men. Don't do it darling, I need you for my own! I'll find a way back to you somehow, I promise! Dad's been going on and on at me about how useless I am and threatening to put me into any job that pays a living wage however much I hate the idea. The trouble is that, as you know, any reasonable job is hard to come by these days, and I know that he and Mum are pretty hard up. If I'm honest, I know they have a right to be fed up with me, when I had such a chance and then threw it away. But somehow they never seemed to have any real purpose in their own lives. They've always talked about earning more money to buy a bigger car or a colour TV or something. I mean, I'm still asking, 'So what, what's the point anyway if you're not happy?' They never seem to have enough – it's as if money's some sort of god to them – but here I am, having to live off their reluctant charity or worse still, on the dole and having to admit I can't even afford to come down and see you, let alone live in London! So I just don't know what's right any more. When I get like this I always feel how easy it would be just to end it all – if it wasn't for you, I wouldn't hesitate. Look after yourself for me darling.

All my love,
XXXXJOHN. XXXX

March 7th. Croydon

Darling,

I'm so sorry to have been so long in writing but I haven't known quite what to say. You weren't here & I was at my wits end about what to do, & I've made the most terrible mess of things. I suppose I'll have to tell you before some other 'kind' person does. Just after I wrote last time, I felt really, really ill. It had been coming on for some time, but I was so depressed about us I didn't know how much was real & how much I was imagining. Anyway, I went home for the weekend – only because I absolutely had to after about 8 weeks away – & Mum took one look at me & marched me straight off down to the family doctor. It didn't take him long to discover what I had already more than my suspicions about – that I was well & truly pregnant. Although I was nearly sure myself, it was awful to hear the words, & of course my parents were absolutely furious. They went on & on at me, about what a disgrace it was to the family name, what a little slut I was & how they'd never understand me & so on. I wanted to scream out – what about me, what about our baby, don't <u>we</u> matter? It just seemed as if the only thing that concerned them was what the neighbours might think & how inconvenient it all was for them. I just longed for you to talk it all over with, darling. There was no one else in the whole wide world who could possibly understand, but Dad wouldn't even hear of me ringing you. Then I thought of all the trouble you were in already, & I realised what a worry it would be for you at this time, & there was honestly nothing you could do to help me anyway. So I just gave up & let them get on with it. The doctor arranged for me to have an abortion as soon as possible. It all sounded so simple – a neat quick operation, over in a few minutes, you feel as good as new again, as if nothing had happened. I'm not sure if I believed him, but I was so desperate I was beyond caring. I did try to mention the possibility of having the baby & keeping it to my parents, but they were so unbelievably horrified I didn't dare pursue the subject. There was nowhere to go,

& no one to help. Darling, I'm <u>so</u> sorry. It was our baby & I feel so terrible about it now. I don't know how to write about the experience, there aren't any words to describe it, but I've cried for days & days, & it feels as if I've lost something desperately precious which is irreplaceable. I never thought much about life before, but that little being was alive, & very much a part of our love, & I've let them murder it. I've never felt so guilty in my whole life before. Often I wake up in the night & feel as if it's still there growing, then the whole horrible truth comes flooding in on me & I can hardly bear it.

My parents have been going on & on at me & treating me like a very wicked girl, & no one ever comes to the house to see me. I haven't been to work for ages, though I have to go back & face them soon. But today an extraordinary thing happened. Do you remember that strange, rather peaceful girl I told you about at the office? Well, she suddenly appeared on the doorstep. It never occurred to me to ask her how she knew where I lived, or why she'd come to see me, but there she was, & I was never more pleased to see anyone in my life. I just couldn't help it. The minute I saw her I burst into tears, but she didn't seem at all surprised, just put her arm around me & led me quietly to the sitting room, & shut the door. My parents were out, thank goodness. It was extraordinary, just as if she understood & accepted everything. I found myself telling her all about us, all about the abortion, &, well, I didn't have to tell her about how awful I felt of course – She just listened & I felt a strange sort of warmth coming from her. I must say I expected her to tell me what a fool I had been, or how dreadful I was (people say she's a bit religious!), but she only seemed to care about <u>me</u> & what I was going to do. She didn't preach at me or anything like that. It was such a relief after my parents going on & on at me – I wanted to cry again, just because at long last somebody was prepared to accept me for myself, & not just see the terrible mess I'm in.

But darling, I am terribly frightened about us all of a sudden! I'm so confused I don't know what to think! I just don't know how you will feel about our baby, or about me, any more. Part of me is even angry with you. Why did you do this to me? Where were you when I needed you? And then just saying that makes me feel guilty, when you're in the mess you're in. I need to see you quickly, & yet I'm afraid to. Where are we going from here? What's happening to us?

Please write to me soon & tell me what to do. Tell me you still love me.

Lots of love,
Jackie. xx

Gareloch March 9th.

Dearest Jackie,

I'm so very sorry about what's happened, and like I said before, I know it's all my fault for talking you into it. And I really feel bad that I wasn't there to help you and to stand alongside you at the time. But, darling, you need to relax, too, and look at things calmly. Don't be so hard on yourself, on both of us, if it comes to that – when all's said and done you did the only thing you could do in the circumstances I suppose these things do happen; and it's sad, but you mustn't let yourself be so guilty! We took precautions that didn't work out, that's all. Darling, I know you're feeling dreadful, but think – you're still worn out physically by the operation, and that's making you react like this. You've got to be positive about it now, for both our sakes. After all, lots of girls have abortions these days and get over them – think how much worse it would be to have to go ahead and have the baby – I mean for you Jackie. You'd be tied down and miserable, probably more miserable than you are now: you're too young for that kind of responsibility. And as for the practical problems — how could we support a family? – I mean, I can hardly support myself right now. I'm sure that when you're over the emotional harm all this sort of thing does to you you'll feel quite differently about it all.

And Jackie, of <u>course</u> I feel just the same about you, and I wish you weren't so far away. I really would love to come down and help you, but now that I haven't got the flat anymore it's just not that easy! Right now it's even harder for me to come down – I've got a job – through a mate of Dad's, selling cars for a sort of dealer. It's not bad, but I've really got to stick at it if I'm going to get anywhere, and that means staying around here. The money's good though, and I'm saving up, so I'll be down to see you sometime, which is great. The guy I'm working for's generous with the job perks, too. He let me borrow the best machine in the showroom the other night to take some of my friends up to the loch. We had a really good time! Of course it would have been much better if you'd been here, but then, as I said we've both got to keep living, or else we'll go crazy!!

Darling, I still love you _very_ much. Just get over this thing as soon as you can and everything will be O.K., you'll see.

Lots of love,

John.

Croydon March 11th.

Dear John,

I feel really mad at you after that letter! After all I've been through, all you can say is, 'Oh you'll get over it,' & 'how terrible it would be to have a baby around at your age.' Lots of people get married at my age. It doesn't seem to worry you at all that we have started a baby & then killed it. I read an article in a magazine at the doctor's – too late unfortunately – saying that even at a few weeks old the foetus is alive & conscious in the womb. So if you look at it that way it's a little short of murder! And this was a child born of _our_ love. I can still hardly bear to think of it myself. How callous can you men get?

I did hope that at least you would _try_ to come down to see me. It wasn't _much_ to ask if you really love me!

I can't understand it – you never found it difficult to get anywhere you wanted to before. Suddenly it's all too much hassle; now you've got a reasonable job & you feel better, it's up to me to hurry up & feel better too, no matter how bad I'm feeling!

I <u>can't</u> get over what you said in that letter. When I think of all the lovely, caring things you used to say to me when we were lying in bed together, how you seemed to just take over my life & help me with everything that came up. Was this because you were getting what you wanted from me? Or was it because you were here & not 500 miles away? I <u>still</u> can't believe the way you just calmly say, 'you'll get over it'!! John, it just isn't the you I used to know.

An abortion isn't quite so simple as you seem to think you know! O.K. so you've lost the trouble of worrying about my having a baby (or were you afraid I might expect you to marry me right away?) But something inside of <u>me</u> is utterly wretched.

I lie awake at night feeling empty & cold, & sometimes I dream about the child beginning to move around inside me & then wake up expecting to find it still there. Something seems to have started in my body that feels unfinished — lost for ever. I even wanted to know what the child would have looked like, to let it grow & see the fruit of our love together. Now it almost seems as if destroying the child has destroyed our love as well. I know I could never feel the same about our sleeping together again.

~~Honestly~~ darling, reading your letter makes me wonder who my real friends are. My boss has been really super — he's letting me come back after 3 weeks leave, no questions asked. (I think Jenny, the girl I told you about, had a hand in that, because he never even mentioned my trouble!) And Jenny herself has been wonderful. She rings me up every day to see how I'm getting on, & let's me know that she's thinking about me. If I'm feeling low or miserable she lets me flow on & just accepts whatever I say. She doesn't criticise or tell me to snap out of it. If she is religious then all I can say is she doesn't ram her views down my throat! Sometimes I would really like to know what makes her tick. None of my other friends seem to have bothered about me very much, & my parents have driven away anyone who has tried, so I would have been very alone otherwise.

Talking about Jenny makes me wonder about you John. I know it sounds irrational & I can just hear you asking what I mean, but I do long for you to be more loving when I need you so desperately! I *know* most men don't understand how a girl feels at this sort of time, but all the same your attitude hurts me deep inside. Whatever happened to all the wonderful feelings & concerns you used to have about me?

Please write to me John, & tell me you do really care, & that all these feelings I've got aren't true. I need you so much, & I hate the feeling of the distance that separates us. Whatever is happening to us?

Lots of love,

Jackie.

P.S. Please write soon xxxxxxxxxxxxx

March 14th.
Gareloch

Dearest Jackie,

I *do* care, honestly I do. I'm just not good at putting it down on paper. I didn't realise how much an abortion hits a girl. Talking to one of my work mates the other day about his girl-friend in the same situation made me realise that it very often happens like you've said. I do wish I could have been there to help you, and I'm really sorry that I wasn't.

Honestly darling, now that it's all over though I can't see the point of rushing down to see you. We'd have so little time to be together it would just make things worse for both of us. You've got this friend Jenny to help you, and I'm really glad about that, it's good to know she's there. (But watch out if she is religious – for heaven's sake don't let her turn you into one of those 'holier than thou' sorts who call themselves Christians. They seem to have a down on all the pleasures of life as far as I can see. It's O.K., that's meant to be a joke, but you know what I mean!)

Yes, I suppose I was afraid that actually having a baby would force us to get married right away, and although you know I love you, Jackie, I'm not really ready to settle down and get married just yet. I mean it <u>was</u> <u>wonderful</u> living with you, but I couldn't feel happy tied down to married life and all its responsibilities! I mean, can you imagine me as a father?! And anyway I've got to work this job up into something good before we can begin to afford to get married. I know you always said we could manage on a shoestring, but I'm beginning to learn the hard way that you've got to be responsible about these things. We've got to be able to afford to set up some kind of a home before we can even think about marriage. I mean, I know I've always despised Dad for talking like that about life, but now that I'm faced with the situation myself, I can see he's right. Money matters more than you think. I still miss you darling, very much, and life isn't the same without you around, but we'll just have to be patient and wait. Things are looking up job-wise already. I sold 15 cars last week, and they are talking about up-grading my pay next month. I'll be able to afford to come down and see you in a month or two when I can get some leave.

Lots of love, JOHN.

March 20th. Croydon

Dear John,

I feel as if something is dying. Now that you are so far away, your world is a completely different one. All the time that we were together you talked so much about hating your parents' attitude towards money, their empty lives, their preoccupation with material things, 'having a tidy sum in the bank', 'saving up for a new car', 'recognising your material responsibilities' & so on.

I can hear you now, laughing about it & making fun of their values; saying how futile & empty their lives were; saying that it would never be like that for us, that we would live for better things.

I remember as though it were only last week, the wonderful feeling of togetherness we had. As if we had our own little world & nothing else mattered. All right I know people have to be responsible, but we were living on very little _then_ & it did'nt seem to matter! Suddenly now your whole world seems to centre on money & saving up, & this _marvellous_ new job you've got. Tell me .... how many months does it take to save up the train fare from Scotland, not to mention the coach or hitchhiking. Or now that your world is centred on money, will there ever be enough by your standards for anything, let alone getting married?

You tell me not to get too affected by Jenny's religion, but all I can say is, give me her values & her friends any day, rather than the money-minded bunch you seem to have landed up with! Last weekend she drove me over to spend the day with her family & some of her friends from church. I was a bit apprehensive after what you'd said, & as you know I've always had a thing about long-faced, pious church-goers, too. But honestly, I couldn't have been more *wrong*!

Her family were quite extraordinary & really good fun. They seem to keep open house to any one of their own, or their children's friends, & people came & went all day. I felt immediately accepted by them, like one of the family. Just as I felt when I first got to know Jenny.

And as for her brothers & her friends, well, it was *amazing* – they were just so normal, & yet there they were saying grace at mealtimes as if it were the most natural thing to do, & then carrying on as if nothing had happened. Occasionally God came up in conversation as if he were a normal presence around the place, & I almost expected to turn around & catch a glimpse of him, or see a light shining somewhere! It was very strange to me, but very natural just the same.

We had a friendly table tennis championship, & then went for a long drive in a strange variety of wayout, & somewhat battered, cars out to the South Downs.

chug! chug!

We went for a mad walk together in the twilight, throwing last year's soggy fallen leaves at one another. Their happiness was infectious, & after a while I felt better just for being with them. There was a hint of spring in the air, & something began to stir in me again — the feeling that it was good to be alive after all.

When I left they were talking about church next morning, & you won't believe this, but I <u>really</u> wanted to go with them! Unfortunately I couldn't, because my mother had gone & asked some of our most boring relatives over for the day, & my presence helping with all the dreary & unnecessary chores before lunch was necessary. She gets so worked up if I'm not in attendance to help. Honestly, coming home after the Williams' household is the most terrible anticlimax. Everything has to be done the right way, nothing matters except what people think of you. 'Auntie Flo expects you to be here. I hope she doesn't know what has happened to you recently or she would never speak to you again.' (Frankly, who cares?) 'Cousin George is such a nice boy. If only you had gone out with him when he asked you, you wouldn't be in this mess now."

I really think that if I'd stayed at home without Jenny's help after the abortion I should have gone stark raving mad. They scarcely spoke to me, & eyed me with critically disapproving looks whenever I appeared. Even Dad, who I always thought had a soft spot for me, seemed to withdraw into his shell, as if I had suddenly become some sort of monster! I suppose Mum terrorised him into submission. I only wish he had the strength of his own convictions & stood up to her! Oh, maybe I'm being unfair, but they are so horrified by this abortion thing that they don't know how to handle it all! Grandma was pretty strict with Mum when she was young, so I suppose that's part of the trouble.

Still, if it hadn't been for Jenny taking the trouble to come round so often, I really don't know how I would have coped. It was bad enough trying to get over what had happened, without their icy wall of disapproval & rejection! I can just begin to see it for what it was now, but immediately after the abortion it was simply awful, & I would have sooner killed myself than gone on living like that!

Thank goodness they have grudgingly come to accept Jenny, & even seem to like her. I doubt if th would approve of the Williams' household, or the happy-go-lucky way they live. I can just *see* my mother keeping open house like that! But Jenny is good with them, & even Mum quickly thawed out when she spent half an hour helping her to weed the front garden the other day. But then my parents don't know about her religious tag, & like you, they certainly wouldn't approve of that. 'It doesn't do to get involved with all this church nonsense.' Occasionally one can go for a nice Christmassy feeling, & of course a church wedding is better than a registry office. 'After all, it's what the relatives & neighbours expect, isn't it?' 'People don't like to think you're getting religious, & it's so important to make the right impression, isn't it?!

She's rattled on like that for years, & I'm beginning to see, in the cold light of my own experience now, just how much it's really worth. Nothing but appearances matter, & life at home is like an empty shell.

I'm sorry John, I seem to have written an awful lot about home & the Williams's, but that's my life at the moment, & I don't know what else to say to you. Lying in bed at night I often think of those lovely months we had together, & long for your warmth beside me, but even as I do that, I have the feeling that something has gone that can never be the same again!

All your talk about marriage — about not wanting to be tied down, needing to save up, & so on, has made me wonder just how much our relationship is really worth. I thought you'd lived with me long enough to know that I'm not worried about having savings in the bank, or being able to go to expensive places. Often we've been very happy just knocking up an omelet or opening a tin, & quietly sitting listening to records together I really never dreamed that you would change so suddenly into someone for whom money would matter so much as to stand in the way of our happiness together. It doesn't even sound in your letter as if you want to be married anymore! I felt really depressed & miserable last week after your letter came on Thursday morning. I just didn't know how to answer it. But now after the weekend, suddenly so much seems to be changing for me. It's as though a new door in my life is starting to open, & I actually want to know what happens on the other side.

I still miss you terribly John, & I don't want what seems to be happening to us. Why couldn't you have been there when I needed you so much?

Lots of love
Jackie.

Gareloch March 24th.

Dearest Jackie,

I was really upset after reading your letter and still can't realise what it is I've said, or not said, that has made things change so much for you!

We agreed _ages_ ago that we loved each other so much we would get married one day. I only left you to come back to Scotland because I had to leave college, and I _keep saying_ how much I miss you! What more do you want? You _know_ that work is hard to come by these days, and I'm really lucky to have got this job. Of course you could come up to join me, but I really don't feel I'm fit for it yet. Would it help to buy you an engagement ring? A sort of a promise for some time in the future?

You were always so giving and easy to be with, never making any demands on me. I'm afraid you've caught me a bit out of my depth on this abortion thing. I really had no idea it was _so_ bad for you! I'm sure you would feel differently about it if I were nearer and could come over and spend time with you. You still seem to think it's easy enough from Scotland, but it's very difficult as I have to work Saturday mornings, and right now I really don't want to rock the boat. Things are going so well I can hardly believe it, and I don't want to start asking for extra days off and things until I've really been accepted as an essential part of the firm. I promise you we'll both benefit in the end – you'll see what a difference a bit of money makes in life. It's all very well your making scathing comments about my parents! I know I _used_ to talk about them like that, but they've been very good to me over this last trouble, and I'm beginning to see how right they were about lots of things I used to attack before.

There are certain things you just have to get together before you can settle down — not just material things either. You've got to be mature about it all. The trouble is that living on a grant at college is like a cloud-cuckoo land, protected from the hard realities of life outside, and — well, I've just been down with a bump once and I don't want another one, that's all!

I'm getting awfully tired of hearing about this Jenny person and her family too. What's so special about them? After all it's easy enough for her to come over or ring up every day if she only lives a few minutes away, and you work in the same office, too. Anyone would think they were some fantastic band of neo-angels the way you go on about them. And one thing I warn you, when we do get married, don't go on at me about any of the religious stuff; I had quite enough of that in R.E. at school to last me a lifetime!!

Honestly Jackie, I can't see that anything has changed in our relationship. It's just that we've been through a bit of trouble, and we are too far apart to see one another. That's bound to make you feel a bit low until we're together again. I really do love you darling, and I need you so much; please don't talk as though things are breaking up — I couldn't bear that. Just get stuck into your work again and forget about everything that's happened. That's the best way. Soon you'll see we'll be as close as we were before. I'm counting on you darling.

Lots of love,

John. XXXX

Croydon March 28th.

Darling John,

Thank you so much for your letter. It certainly helped me get things much more sorted out in my mind. I felt I could begin to hope again that you really do care after all!

O.K., I know I'm probably being unreasonable about your job & your responsibilities. Of course it's true you can't let your parents down *again* after failing at college, losing your grant & all that. I just *hurt* inside still, & it feels as if you are the only person who could make it better. Just letting myself think about you makes me long to have your arms around me, comforting me & telling me it's all right. I need to *hear* you say you still love me & nothing has changed.

I'm feeling pretty desperate again at the moment – it's almost as bad as it was just after the abortion. Apparently this sometimes happens about a month afterwards – I just hope it's the last time though. I really can't cope with these awful empty aching feelings *all over again*! Anyway, I have managed to save up a bit of my money this past 3 months, & they have been very good not cutting my pay when I was away. How would you feel if I came up to see you for a few days next month? I am sure I could find somewhere to stay, sort of bed & breakfast, if there wasn't room for me at your place & you feel it's difficult with your parents. I can't go on like this needing you & never seeing you, so this really seems the only answer, if you can't get away with your job, meaning working on Saturdays. If I take the whole Easter holiday, & a couple of extra days unpaid, I'm sure they would understand. I could come up by coach & be with you the best part of a week. What do you feel about the idea?

Just thinking about it makes me feel better already! I do hope you think it's O.K.? I was afraid to suggest it before because I wasn't sure whether you really wanted me around, or even if you still cared about me! This abortion thing has knocked me <u>so much</u> that sometimes I don't quite know what is real & what is not. I get low & very depressed like this at the moment for no apparent reason. I can see it's much easier for me to come to you, rather than sit here & expect you to do all the travelling with your present job. It was just that I was feeling <u>so unsure</u> of myself until I got your last letter.

Please write soon & tell me what you think about the idea.

Lots of LOVE,

Jackie.

Gareloch March 31st

Darling Jackie,

It was *so* lovely to get your letter and hear you sound much more like your old self, even if things are getting you down again at the moment. I was feeling terrible after your last one. I was really begining to be afraid I was losing you.

I think it's a wonderful idea your coming up at Easter, and I just can't wait to see you again. One of my friends lives in a bed and breakfast place about half a mile from here, and says the woman who runs it is quite decent.

He is going to ask her if she'd have room that week. Some of them are bound to be away over the holiday.

For my part, you know I'd love to have you here, but my parents are a bit edgy about us still. I am afraid they blame you for my failing my exams at college, which I know is quite unfair, but you know what parents are like. Also, they're not used to people staying in the house, or even visiting come to that. They'd be so uptight about having you, or anyone, around, that it would be <u>sheer misery</u> for both of us! If you have your own room over at Mrs. McTavish's that would be much better in every way.

I've got so many plans in my mind already about what we can do when you're here. We can get a car from work and drive up to the hills beyond Loch Lomond. There's a lovely little stream up there with lots of quiet places along the banks.

Then I would love to take you up into the Highlands another day. Of course I'll have to work some of the time but perhaps they'd let you come into the showrooms a bit. So long as we stay away from my parents it's going to be great. I just mentioned the possibility of your coming up to see me last night over supper, and there was a sort of frozen silence. Oh well, I'm just not going to take any notice. They can't *run* my life!

Darling, just go ahead with those plans as *quickly as possible*, and let me know what time you'll be arriving and when to meet you! I love you *very much* and it will be wonderful to see you again!

All my love

John. x♡xxx

APRIL 3rd. Croydon

Darling John,

I feel so happy after getting your letter. Suddenly the world is a better place to be in, & I know you love me just as much as you always did. Also I'm feeling much better inside which certainly helps.

I've not got much time to write now because it's just my lunch break, but I thought I'd write quickly to let you know my plans. I'll be coming up on the coach that gets into Glasgow Terminal, wherever that is, about 10.00 am. Saturday morning. I had quite a job to get a seat over the holiday, but luckily they've just had a couple of cancellations. If you can't get away to meet me then I can probably get a bus out to Gareloch from the terminal. Just let me know. Only a few more days!

It seems too good to be *true*!

All my love darling,

Jackie.

Gareloch April 5th.

Dearest Jackie,

Getting an hour off to meet you at the terminal; I hope this letter gets to you on time. I'm so longing to see you it's really wonderful!

All my love

John. ☺

April 18th. Croydon

Darling John,

That was a wonderful week in so many ways, & yet for me a rather sad one.

It was so lovely to see you again, waiting for me as the coach pulled in. Funny, but I felt almost shy with you after all this time. To have been so close & then not to have seen you again for two whole months! But just feeling your arms around me made me feel so very happy again.

I had so much to say to you & yet it seemed so difficult to talk at first. All the usual things seemed so trivial after all that had gone on between us. All the time I couldn't help looking back & longing for the days when we spent so much time together in the flat. It all seemed so much more real, more natural, then. For a while I wished I hadn't come. It was like waking up from a beautiful dream to the cold, clear light of day.

But <u>thank you</u>, darling, for taking so much time & trouble over the week, & for all the wonderful things you planned for us to do. I just loved being up by that little stream in the hills; our own private bank with the smell of the pine trees & the flash of primroses along the stream. It was good just to sit & be silent with you holding me in your arms, to feel your warmth close to me again.

It was great driving with you in the car too, to see how much enjoyment you were getting from it, & how well your job was going. I can absolutely understand it now, darling, you seemed happier than I've seen you for a long time. More as if you've really found something to work for & enjoy. College always seemed such a strain on you, as though it was something your parents had pushed you into, but that wasn't really you!

I felt sad though that you didn't even suggest my meeting your parents at all, & they didn't apparently ask to see me. Somehow it made everything seem very hole-in-the-cornerish. I can absolutely understand your not wanting me to stay there, but I would like to have seen them _just once_ after coming all that way! It makes me wonder too, with all your talk of getting married one day, just when you're going to be prepared to face telling them about it. After all, I've had to face much heavier issues with my parents recently! They were hardly over-joyed at the idea of my coming up to see you, & have been icy, to say the least, since my return.

Then there's the other thing. Did you really expect me to sleep with you again so soon, after all that's happened to me recently? When you got round to the subject so quickly, & seemed to have little else on your mind, I could hardly believe it! You don't seem to have understood a thing I have written about, or any of the pain or inner heart-break I have been through at all!

Of course there was a part of me that longed to as well! You can't live like that for so long & not want to return to it again. But I thought that you of all people would understand what I'd been through, & make allowances for how I was feeling. I still feel terribly guilty, John, about the abortion, that it was a kind of murder for which we are both in our own way responsible. I _still_ can hardly forgive myself, let alone expect anyone else to. So how on earth do you think I could so quickly & so thoughtlessly risk putting myself into the same situation again how ever many precautions we took? I would still feel terribly guilty at the thought of enjoying sex again, at least for a while, or until we were married, or, at the very least, finally engaged.

What hurts most of all, is that you didn't think of this. That despite all your protestations of sympathy & concern, you scarcely seem to have thought it through from my angle at all! You were genuinely surprised & hurt that I didn't see Mrs. McTavish's bed-sitter as the perfect opportunity, & even more astonished when I left without finally giving way to your pleading! It just seems to me that if you _really_ loved me deeply at all you would never even have asked this of me at such a time.

Or did you _ever_ love me like that? Perhaps our whole relationship was built on sex. We certainly got into it pretty quickly to begin with, against my better judgement! It's as if we founded our togetherness on this, & nothing else, so that when we were just together as friends this time it wasn't enough. There was nothing to keep us close.

And darling, unless we were to get married right away almost, it doesn't seem to me there is anything else to keep us together, & even then I wonder. How much do any couple have going for them in today's world when their whole relationship is built on sex & sex alone? We can't sit for ever gazing into each other's eyes & holding each other close. Living is about other things as well!

ρ ρ ρ ρ ρ

I left you on Sunday feeling sad & empty. Not because we hadn't slept together, though that was obviously uppermost in <u>your</u> mind, but because it seemed to me that something had gone for ever. Perhaps just a dream, but a beautiful dream just the same. I saw what I didn't want to see, & perhaps what I was afraid of all along—how much our relationship was really worth.

Perhaps it's only a result of all that has happened to us in the meantime, so that we have both grown up to see, in different ways, that yesterday was a waking dream. You are having to think about money & work & responsibilities, & fair enough, that's a part of life you have to consider – though I wish we'd considered it before we rushed headlong into living together as if nothing else mattered!

I have woken up from my dream to see there is a great deal more to life than two people being close & having sex together. I feel guilty, unclean, cheated of something, & aware that there are more important things in life than we have found in our relationship together, though there _was_ a time not so long ago when I used to think that we had everything I could possibly wish for. I kept finding myself wanting something more from you, some strength or direction, a meaning to life that I can't find on my own. I don't know what I'm saying really, except that whatever it is, or was, between us has gone for me. I hope this letter doesn't hurt you, darling. I was so aware all the time I was with you that you didn't _begin_ to understand all that was going on for me, & I didn't know how to make you see.

But John, thank you for the week, & for all you still mean to me.

With love,

Jackie.

Gareloch April 23rd.

Dearest Jackie,

Your letter makes me very sad. I could see something was going on for you but I couldn't understand what. I don't suppose I'd thought much about sleeping together before you arrived. I just assumed that as we had always done this before we'd go on doing it, and then when I saw you again and held you close it was the most wonderful feeling, and that made me long even more to go back to bed with you as we'd always done. And all the time you so obviously didn't want to do this I felt hurt, rejected. Nothing seemed complete any more, and I began to wonder if you really loved me at all.

I can try to see it from your point of view, but it's very difficult for me. O.K. so I suppose there's one chance in a thousand that you might get pregnant again, but it just seems to me our relationship is more important. Of course I don't want you to go through all that again, though I can't feel the same guilt that you obviously do about it, and neither can I see the slightest likelihood of your having to do so. It seems that this wretched abortion thing has done something terrible to us. Suddenly it's all dust and ashes, and we have to start building again on the heap of rubble that's left.

Sleeping together was an essential part of our relationship, at least it was for me, and I can't forget all about it just like that. Furthermore, I don't see what's so wrong with that statement. Thousands of people sleep together all over the country, and they seem to get by perfectly happily. After all, it's the same as you do when you're married isn't it?

Saying that you couldn't do it again until we're actually married is really putting pressure on me, too. I've already told you I can't possibly consider this until I have saved up enough for us to get a flat together. My parents would go crazy at the very suggestion.

We could get engaged it's true, but it would have to be a long engagement and could be difficult now we're so far apart.

Like you I just don't know what's happening to us, and I wish with all my heart that this wretched abortion thing had never been necessary. You say you keep wanting more from me like strength or direction and a meaning to life. That's really asking for <u>something</u>— I don't even know where I'm going myself! All we had was our close relationship together, and now I don't know what is happening to <u>that</u> even. Please help me Jackie, and try to be more reasonable. I still love you very much.

LOTS OF LOVE, John.

Croydon April 28th.

Dearest John,

I feel numb now after that Easter week with you. It's as if something that was an essential part of my life is slipping away from me fast, & I can't do anything about it, however much I want to.

It's horrible being home again, & my parents have been getting worse by the hour. They hardly speak to me & are obviously shattered by the fact that I even _wanted_ to see you again, let alone that I actually went up all the way up to see you, for what they imagine was a 'week of sin.' If only they knew! Maybe they are really concerned for my welfare but all they talk about is what the neighbours think!

But Jenny has been wonderful, thank goodness. All right, I can just hear you moaning! But she has been the one bright spark in my life down here all this time, & I don't know what I would have done without her. Next week I'm moving out to share a flat with a friend of hers near the office, & I simply can't wait to get out of here. It will be wonderful to be independent again. I really have tried with my parents because I felt I owed them something after all that's happened. They said they wanted me to stay at home so I gave it a try & let my place in the old flat go, but honestly it's been living hell; watching the box every night, complaining if I didn't spend every evening with them, criticising my every move & everything I wear, as if they owned me body & soul! It would be different if there were some freedom or reality around the place like in the William's home, for instance, but here it's like being in a cage where the zoo keepers simply take a distant interest. I'm sure they probably mean well underneath, but I don't have any real relationship with either of them.

I do understand how you feel about sleeping together, darling. It's just that I wanted you to be more understanding, more sympathetic about my present state! Like you I don't know if I could stand a long engagement if we were miles apart, & if we were close to each other we would still have that problem, I just can't get rid of this feeling of guilt. It's strange to you maybe, but it's very real to me just the same.

We seem to be caught in some kind of a trap of our own making, & one that there's no way out of. I only wish our relationship had developed more slowly to start with, then I'm sure we wouldn't be in this mess now. The trouble is how do we go back? How do I get rid of this feeling of the wrong we've done & the barrier that stands between us? Anyway darling, thank you for your letter, & for at least *trying* to understand.

Lots of love,

JACKIE

Gareloch 3rd May.

Darling Jackie,

Thank you so much for your letter. I feel happier already receiving it. I'm so glad you're moving out of your parents' place into a flat again. That's bound to make things better for you. I can't imagine why you let them persuade you to stay at home in the first place, but then I suppose I can't talk!

I hope we won't ever turn into parents like ours. It's this grotesque business of never being free to be oneself; always having to do things their way, or as you say, 'to please the neighbours.'

All I want is for them to accept me as me, but somehow nothing is ever right. That's really why I didn't risk bringing you here when you were staying at Mrs. McTavish's. It's not that I don't want you to meet them, darling. They've never approved of <u>any</u> of my friends and it doesn't seem worth the effort of bringing up yet another problem until we have to. I suppose I am a bit of a coward at heart, but if I have to live at home I would rather have an easy life with them than these endless arguments.

I'm sorry your parents have been so difficult, darling. I'm afraid I never thought of that for you. One way and another I do seem to have been rather wrapped up in my own problems through all your troubles and I haven't been much good for you. I can see that now. It isn't intentional, dearest, please believe me.

I'm saving up now to come down to see you. It won't be long before I have been here long enough to get a bit of time off, and then I'll be able to come. Please hang on to our love until we meet again, darling. I'm sure we can start again and that everything will be all right; you'll see.

Lots of love,

John.

London 8th May

Dearest John,

I moved into this flat with Leslie & Jane at the end of last week & what a difference it makes to life! I feel so much better already!

It's a really nice place, a bit old & ramshackle, but full of character, & they have decorated it in lovely bright colours, with plenty of posters around the place. They're really great people, too. Not at all like the girls at work; fun to be with, & yet really concerned about other people, if you know what I mean. Leslie is an old friend of Jenny's, & Jane goes to the same church. It's funny but they have the same sort of attitude to life as the Williams.

You feel that life is there to be lived, & not at other people's expense either. There's that same feeling of a 'presence' around the place too; the odd poster on the wall that says 'My peace be with you', & 'God so loved the world that He gave His Son for us'. I've seen that sort of thing before on buses & outside ancient-looking, decrepit churches & it's made me feel slightly sick, but <u>here</u> it sort of fits into the atmosphere – it does feel <u>like</u> that – peaceful, giving & real.

O.K. I know you've heard enough about that! I can just imagine what you'll say in reply, but I only wish you could see it for yourself. It would be lovely if you could come down & see me sometime soon, darling. I do *so* understand about your parents. I didn't realise quite how much home was getting me down until I got out of it.

Lots of love
Jackie.

Gareloch 14th May.

Dearest Jackie,

Not again! I thought we'd got rid of all that religious stuff! Now that you've finally moved in with that lot I suppose we shall *never* hear the end of it. We're in the space age now you know, and things like Adam and Eve and all those Bible Myths just don't *fit* any more. Surely you must see that! My friends would laugh themselves silly if I even *mentioned* the subject, let alone suggested that I might believe in it all! We're on our own down here you know. No cosy old Father God in the sky like a benign Santa Claus watching over us.

Take a look at some of the suffering and unemployment around you, and you'll see what I mean. Where's your God in all that?

If I come down to see you I want to see you *by yourself* and *not* with that lot! At any rate I'm not so naive as you, and I wouldn't be taken in by all this atmosphere stuff. Now just forget about it, please. I'm serious about that. I love *you*, not your friends.

Lots of love,

John.

London 18th May.

Darling John,

You really don't begin to understand do you? O.K. I know you were brought up with all this hard line Scots' religion without a drop of fun or love in it, but that doesn't mean that's the real thing! From what I've seen of God so far that's not at all what he's like. I don't know how to say this, but I'd better take the plunge, so here goes. Last Sunday I did go to church with them all, & to the club afterwards. Thinking about you & all your bitter feelings, nearly kept me away I'll admit, but then I thought, 'He doesn't own me body & soul &, after all, if he's right I'll know soon enough,' so I went.

I hadn't been to church for years, not since my cousin's wedding about three years ago, & that was a complete farce. But this couldn't have been more different. The place was packed to the doors, & we just managed to squeeze in at the side with some friends of Jenny's. And that's another thing; nearly half the people there were our age or younger.

I always thought only old ladies & peculiar people went to church & that's all! The atmosphere was great there too! No horrible awesome hush but a feeling of real friendship & togetherness. People smiled when we came in as if they really were pleased to see us. But anyway, what I'm getting to is this. The service was really great. Lively songs that I hadn't heard before, people singing to a guitar & one guy standing up to say (in front of all those people!) how much becoming a Christian only a few weeks ago had really meant to him. But it was the *talk* that made the difference to me & that's what I want to tell you about.

This man was telling us about the reason Jesus died, & as he said it I felt he was talking to me alone, out of all the people there. He said that God loves me so much that he sent his Son to die for all the wrong things I'd ever done, that no matter what it was, even murder, the death of Jesus had paid the penalty for that sin, & I could lay it at the foot of his cross, & he would take the guilt of it away for ever.

At first, listening, it seemed too good to be true! I just couldn't take this forgiveness.

Having an abortion & killing our own child seems such a terrible thing, that I felt somehow I ought to be made to pay for it, but the man went on to say that no one could ever make up for their wrong doings or be good enough for God's perfect standards, & whether their sins were big or small, this was why Jesus had to die. And so I thought, why not? Why not my sin? If Jesus really did love me that much, & certainly Jenny & her friends have shown me more <u>real</u> love, no strings attached, than anyone I've ever known, then why not take the plunge? I needed <u>so much</u> to be free of that guilt, & it's weighed so heavily on me for so long!

Anyway, I did it! When he had finished speaking he said a prayer for anyone listening who didn't already belong to Jesus & needed that forgiveness, to open their hearts to him, & I said that prayer too, & that's only the beginning, only I'm not sure you really want to hear the rest —

I'm sorry John, but I know as I write this it has to mean goodbye to our relationship, at least for now. Not because <u>I</u> want it, but because I know you will hate the thought of this new way of life that I've found. It makes me sad, not just because it means saying goodbye to you, but also because you haven't the faintest idea what you're missing. Please don't close your mind to it John. You've got so angry whenever I have mentioned it that I'm afraid to say much more – but please open your eyes to the possibility that God is for real, & that he really loves _you_ too.

Remember that Easter week when I said I needed a strength & direction from you, & I begged you to tell me where we were going, & you said you didn't even know yourself? Well, now _I_ know! There isn't any human being alive, however wonderful, who can give us that strength or that reason for being here. But God really _can_!

I've never known such peace of mind & such inner happiness before in my life. And I know something else too — He has got a plan for my life & a plan that's best for me, a plan that will work out. O.K., so the sky is still grey sometimes & it rains & often things go wrong, but now I can laugh at them; there's something more important, something *real* to live for. I really long for the plan to include you, John, & I'll be praying for you— although I know you'll hate even the thought of that! But like I said, you don't know what you're missing ....

Lots of love,

Jackie.